MUSICAL INSTRUMENTS OF THE WORLD

Flutes

M. J. Knight

A⁺

Smart Apple Media

Published by Smart Apple Media
2140 Howard Drive West, North Mankato, Minnesota 56003

Designed by Helen James

Photographs by Corbis (Tony Arruza, Tiziana and Gianni Baldizzone, Derick A.
Thomas; Dat's Jazz, Ric Ergenbright, Werner Forman, John Henley, Wolfgang Kaehler,
Kelly-Mooney Photography, Earl & Nazima Kowall, Bob Krist, LWA-Dann Tardif,
Buddy Mays, Michael Maslan Historic Photographs, Royalty-Free, Michael St. Maur
Sheil, Ariel Skelley, Paul A. Souders, Ted Spiegel, David Turnley, Nik Wheeler),
Photri (US Navy photo by Jessica Davis), Sergio Piumatti, John Walmsley

Printed in Thailand

Library of Congress Cataloging-in-Publication Data

Knight, M. J.
Flutes / by M. J. Knight.
p. cm. — (Musical instruments of the world)
Includes index.
ISBN 1-58340-416-3
1. Flute—Juvenile literature. [1. Flute.] I. Title. II. Musical instruments
(North Mankato, Minn.)

ML935.K55 2004
788.3'19—dc222003070353

First Edition

9 8 7 6 5 4 3 2 1

Contents

Introducing Flutes

Flutes Flutes Flutes

This book is about flutes, which belong to the woodwind family of instruments.

These instruments create a sound when the air inside them vibrates. The player either blows into or across the instrument's mouthpiece to create notes. The sound each instrument makes depends on the length of the instrument. The longer the instrument, the lower the sound.

These Chinese flute players are marching in a parade in Hong Kong.

Most early woodwind instruments were made of wood, but today, many are made of metal or plastic.

You can hear woodwind instruments playing classical music in an orchestra. The woodwind section of an orchestra includes flutes and piccolos, playing alongside clarinets, oboes, bassoons, and sometimes saxophones.

Flutes can be heard playing other types of music, too, such as folk, rock, pop, and jazz.

Children practicing together playing a variety of woodwind instruments.

Early Flutes

The very first flutes were made thousands of years ago, when people lived in caves. The bones of an animal such as a deer or bear were hollowed out, and a sound was made by blowing through them. Soon, people discovered that they could make different notes if they pierced holes in the sides of the bones.

From these early beginnings came many of the flutes people play today. In Central and South America, people made flutes from the tiny bones of birds. Later, flutes were made from clay and wood.

Did You Know?

A 45,000-year-old flute was found in a cave in eastern Europe. It had been made from the leg bone of a bear, had four finger holes, and, amazingly, could still be played!

This flute was carved from an animal bone and has a bird's head at one end.

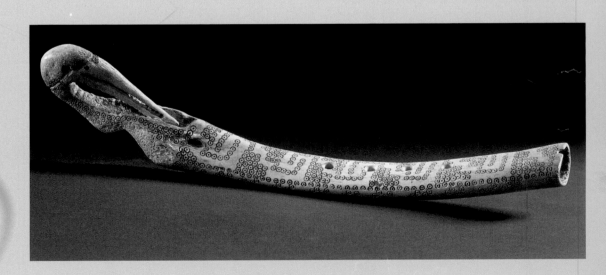

Bird Whistle

Bird Whistle

Bird Whistle

Bird Whistle

Bird Whistle

Bird Whistle

True to its name, this flute makes a low, warbling sound, much like a bird's song.

The bird whistle must be filled with water before it is played. When a player blows down the whistle's spout, the air bubbles through the water and out through a small hole, making a warbling note.

Some bird whistles are made of clay or metal. They can also be made of plastic. Plastic bird whistles make a higher sound.

To play this clay whistle, you fill it with water and blow into the bird's tail.

Tin Whistle

Tin Whistle Tin Whistle Tin Whistle

Another name for the tin whistle is the penny whistle. The name comes from the pennies people used to give musicians who played their instruments in the street.

Tin whistles are made of thin metal. They have six finger holes and no thumb hole, so they are very easy to play.

Some folk bands play lively songs called jigs and reels on tin whistles. The whistles' bright, high sound makes people want to tap their feet and dance.

This tin whistle player is part of a band playing at a music festival in Ireland.

8

Flageolet Flageolet Flageolet

The flageolet is a whistle flute that makes a shrill sound. French and English musicians first played flageolets in bands and orchestras more than 100 years ago. Flageolets were used to play the highest notes in a piece of music.

Early flageolets had a nozzle mouthpiece that held a small piece of sponge. The sponge soaked up the saliva from the player's mouth.

Today, toy flageolets come in many different sizes. They are made of metal but have a plastic mouthpiece.

This toy flageolet has a green plastic mouthpiece and six finger holes.

9

Recorders Recorders

Did you know that there are five different types of recorders? The baby of the family is the sopranino, a tiny recorder with finger holes very close together. Next in size comes the descant recorder, which is the one most often played in schools.

These girls are playing descant recorders at an outdoor concert in the Czech Republic.

You can see the curved metal crook on the bass recorder in the middle of this group. On either side are the tenor and treble recorder.

Treble and tenor recorders are bigger and lower-sounding, but the deepest of all is the bass recorder. It is so big that it has an extra part: a curved metal tube called a crook, which helps players reach the finger holes while blowing.

Recorders have been played in Europe for about 1,000 years. The first recorders were made from a single piece of wood or ivory, but today they are built in three sections and made of wood or plastic.

The soft, clear sound of a recorder is perfect for playing solo pieces or playing in ensembles.

Recorders

11

Nose Flute

Nose Flute Nose Flute

Imagine an instrument you play through your nose! This is exactly how the nose flute is played.

Nose flute playing started in Polynesia, in the Pacific Ocean. Native Polynesians believed that the breath from a person's nose had magic powers.

Nose flute players close one nostril with a finger or a piece of cloth when they play. Their flutes are made of bamboo and have three finger holes that players cover to make different notes.

This Polynesian man holds one nostril closed and blows into his flute through the other one.

Sailors play this tiny metal pipe when welcoming important people aboard ship.

Players hold the pipe in one hand and blow into the mouthpiece. Their breath hits a small hole at the end of the pipe and makes a loud, whistling sound.

To change the note the pipe makes, players open and close their hand. They wear the pipe on a cord around their neck.

This sailor is using her fingers to change the notes she makes with her bosun's pipe.

Ring Flute Ring Flute

The ring flute has a ring of dried palm leaves wrapped around one end. When a player blows into the flute, the ring of leaves helps to direct the breath into the blow hole.

The ring flute comes from Indonesia. Made of bamboo, it has six finger holes and can vary in length. The ring flute is also called the suling. It is usually played in a gamelan orchestra.

The ring flute is often played to accompany special dances in Indonesia.

Double Flute

Double Flute

Double flutes are two flutes in one. Some are carved from one piece of wood, while others are made by tying two pipes tightly together.

Many double flutes come from Eastern Europe. Players can perform two tunes at the same time—one on each pipe. If the pipes are different lengths, they each play a different pitch—one higher than the other.

Ancient flutes made of three or four clay pipes have been found in South America and Mexico. The pipes are joined together so the players' air goes into all of them at the same time.

This double flute player from Rajasthan in India is wearing a traditional red turban.

15

Panpipes
Panpipes
Panpipes

Panpipes are a series of tiny flutes of different lengths joined together in a raft shape. Each pipe plays only one note; the short pipes play higher notes than the long pipes.

Panpipe players blow across the top of each pipe in turn by moving their head or the pipes. The lower end of the pipes is sealed.

Did You Know?

Panpipes were named after a Greek god named Pan. People believed he invented the pipes to play to a goddess he loved named Syrinx.

A piper plays her panpipes by moving the pipes under her lips.

16

Panpipes can be made of clay, stone, wood, metal, or plastic. They are played all over the world. The first panpipes were played in ancient Greece more than 3,000 years ago.

Today, the light, reedy sound of the panpipes is heard most often in South American folk bands. The pipes can be many different sizes. The largest are more than 6.5 feet (2 m) long. They slant away from the player to rest on the ground.

A band of pipers and drummers in Bolivia playing during a farming festival.

Concert Flute

Do you know how many parts a concert flute has? The answer is three: the head joint, the middle joint, and the foot joint. They allow flautists to take the instrument apart, making it easier to carry around.

The mouthpiece in the head joint has a lip plate over a blow hole. Flautists rest their lips on this to play. They blow across, not into, the blow hole to make a note.

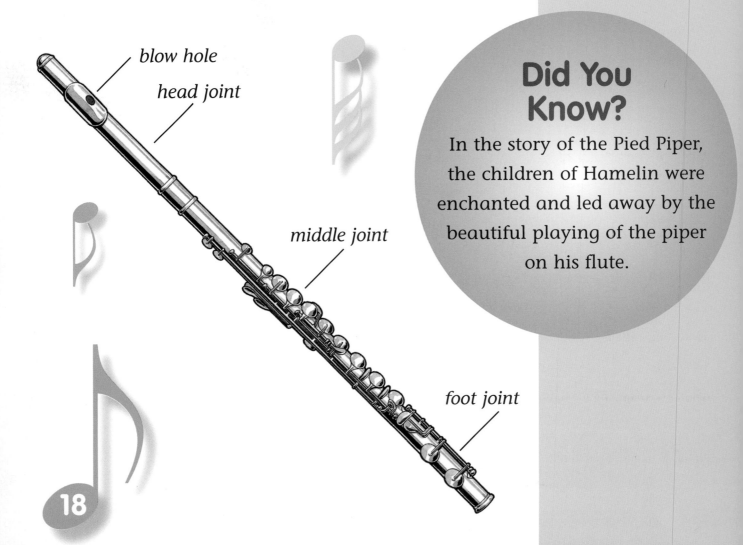

blow hole

head joint

middle joint

foot joint

Did You Know?

In the story of the Pied Piper, the children of Hamelin were enchanted and led away by the beautiful playing of the piper on his flute.

The concert flute has several keys on the middle joint. Flautists hold these down to make different notes.

The concert flute plays in the woodwind section of an orchestra. Its highest notes are strong and bright, while its low notes are full and mellow.

The very first flutes were made of wood, but most flutes today are made of metal—even silver and gold!

These two girls are playing the concert flute in their school band.

Alto Flute and Bass Flute

The alto flute plays sad-sounding notes. It looks like the concert flute, but it is larger and plays deeper notes.

Lower still is the bass flute. This large instrument is very heavy. It is so long that it has to be bent at one end so that flautists can reach all the finger holes.

The alto flute and the bass flute sometimes play in the woodwind section of an orchestra, but they are not usually played as solo instruments.

Did You Know?

If a bass flute was straightened out, it would measure 51 inches (130 cm) long.

This musician is playing the bass flute at a jazz festival.

Piccolo

The baby of the flute family, the piccolo, is just half the size of the concert flute.

The piccolo plays the highest notes in an orchestra. Sometimes it plays a higher version of the tune the violins or flutes are playing. Despite its small size, it has a loud sound that can be heard above all the other instruments.

Piccolo players hold their instrument in the same way as the concert flute and play it by blowing air gently across the blow hole to make a note.

This piccolo player is part of a marching band.

Did You Know?

Piccolo is an Italian word that means "small."

21

Flutes in Concert

The sound of an orchestra is created by many different instruments. They are divided into four sections: strings, woodwind, brass, and percussion.

Flutes play an important part in the woodwind section, which usually has several flutes and at least one piccolo. Flautists sit behind the violas, which are part of the string section. The concert flute often plays the tune in a piece of classical music.

You can also hear the concert flute playing classical music in a wind quintet. This group of five instruments includes a flute, an oboe, a clarinet, a bassoon, and a horn.

These flautists are part of a school concert band.

Flutes can be heard in different types of traditional music, too.

Ti-tzu Ti-tzu Ti-tzu

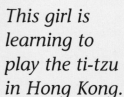

This girl is learning to play the ti-tzu in Hong Kong.

Chinese people have been playing the ti-tzu for thousands of years. It is made of bamboo and played in the same way as a western concert flute: by blowing air across the top of the blow hole.

The ti-tzu has nine finger holes that players cover to make different notes. A small piece of tissue paper stuck over one of the finger holes makes a buzzing sound when the ti-tzu is played.

Did You Know?

The dragon flute is a ti-tzu that is played in religious ceremonies. It has a dragon's head carved at one end and a tail at the other, and is decorated with a shiny substance called lacquer.

23

Ocarina Ocarina Ocarina

The ocarina is an unusual flute because it has a rounded shape, rather than a long, tubular one like most other flutes.

The first ocarinas were probably made in Egypt about 5,000 years ago from bones, baked earth, or large, hollow seeds. Today, many ocarinas are made from clay or plastic.

Did You Know?

The word *ocarina* is Italian for "little goose." The instrument's name comes from the fact that ocarinas in Italy were made in the shape of a bird.

This turtle-shaped ocarina was made by the Aztec people who lived in Mexico hundreds of years ago.

Modern ocarinas are shaped like a long egg. They have a blow hole and up to eight finger holes. Small ocarinas play high notes, and large ones play low notes. The sound is clear and pure.

Some ocarinas have a tuning plunger, which sticks out of one end. The plunger can be pulled out or pushed in to make the instrument play higher or lower notes.

To play the ocarina, you blow into the blow hole and cover the other holes with your fingers.

Ocarinas come in many different shapes and sizes.

Ocarina Ocarina Ocarina

Fife Fife Fife Fife Fife Fife

Fifes are often played in marching bands. These small, narrow, wooden flutes are played in the same way as metal flutes.

Fifes usually have a blow hole and a lip plate, but unlike metal flutes, they cannot be taken apart.

The sound made by a fife is high and shrill, which suits the sort of music that soldiers marched to hundreds of years ago. Fifes are often accompanied by drums.

This boys wears a colonial uniform as he plays the fife as part of a marching band.

26

Swannee Whistle

Swannee Whistle

You pull the plunger in and out to make the swannee whistle's swooping sound.

Have you ever heard a swannee whistle? It makes an amazing "swooping" sound. The sound is made by moving the whistle's plunger.

When players push the plunger into the whistle and blow, the notes slide upward. When players pull the plunger out of the whistle, the notes slide downward.

The swannee whistle has no finger holes and is often played to create a sound effect. It may be heard in music for funny movies or cartoons.

Shakuhachi

Imagine what it would be like to play an instrument while wearing a basket over your head! This is what shakuhachi players had to do long ago. They wore baskets over their heads so that no one would recognize them.

The shakuhachi comes from Japan. It is made from a piece of bamboo cut near the bottom of the plant, where the stem is widest. This gives the shakuhachi a slightly curved shape.

To play the shakuhachi, players rest it on their lower lip and blow against a notch cut into the side of the tube. They make different notes by covering the finger holes.

Today, shakuhachi players perform both classical and folk music on their instruments.

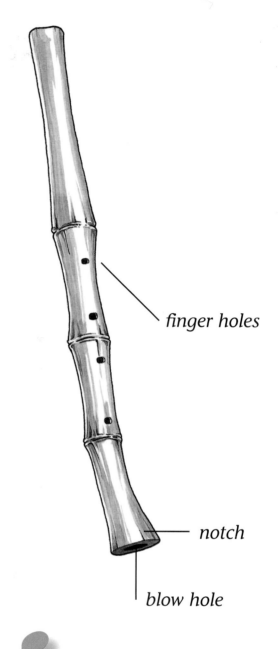

finger holes

notch

blow hole

These Japanese monks are playing their shakuhachis in the traditional way.

Shakuhachi Shakuhachi

Words to Remember

accompanied Played alongside.

bamboo A tall grass with a hollow stem that is used to make many traditional flutes and pipes.

blow hole The name of the hole a flute player blows across to make a note.

classical music Serious music is sometimes called classical music to separate it from popular music. Classical music can also mean music that was written during the late 18th and early 19th centuries and follows certain rules.

crook A long, thin tube on some wind instruments that helps players reach all the finger holes.

ensembles Small groups of musicians who play together.

finger holes The holes in an instrument that the player covers to make different notes.

flautists People who play the flute.

folk Traditional songs and tunes that are so old that no one remembers who wrote them.

gamelan orchestra A group of instruments from Indonesia played in religious ceremonies. It can include percussion instruments, drums, fiddles, and flutes.

jazz A type of music played by a group of instruments in which each one plays its own tune. Jazz musicians often improvise, or make up, the tunes they play.

joint A section of a flute.

keys Small metal caps on a flute that cover the finger holes.

lip plate A rest for the player's lips that helps him or her blow across the blow hole when playing.

marching bands Groups of musicians who march as they play. Most marching bands play music that was originally played by soldiers.

mellow Gentle and warm.

mouthpiece The part of a wind instrument that the player puts to his or her mouth and blows into.

musicians People who play instruments or sing.

notch A cut at the top of some flutes that is shaped like a U or a V. A notch makes the flute easier to play.

orchestra A group of about 90 musicians playing classical music together.

pitch How low or high a sound is.

plunger The rod-like part of a swannee whistle (and some ocarinas) that can be pulled out or pushed in to sound different notes.

pop Popular music that is entertaining and easy to listen to.

reedy Thin and buzzing.

rock Pop music with a strong beat, or rhythm.

shrill High and loud.

solo A piece of music played or sung by one performer.

vibrates Moves up and down very quickly, or quivers. The air inside a wind instrument vibrates when someone blows into it.

Index